NEWS AND

Seven Canadian Poets

Robert Bringhurst
Margaret Avison
Terry Humby
Brent MacKay
Guy Birchard
A.F. Moritz
Alexander Hutchison

Edited by August Kleinzahler

Brick Books
Coldstream

© The Authors, 1982
ISBN 0-919626-17-3
Brick Books, Box 219, Ilderton, Ont. N0M 2A0

CONTENTS

FORWARD

Here are 7 poets I read and listen to with delight. And envy.

Louis Zukofsky said that the test of poetry is the range of pleasure it affords as sight, sound and intellection. I'm not at all sure who could append a nickel's worth to that, though I *am* certain volunteers are legion.

None of these poets is easy. Don't take this book to lunch with you unless it's a very long lunch in a quiet place. Trust that the poet is not bamboozling you, confounding you for no reason, mixing his syntax or strutting his erudition to make you feel the chump. I can tell you that each of these poets writes in dead earnest, and would rather have no reader at all than a smug, lazy one.

A small anthology wants a *very* small introduction. May these seven each win the Irish Sweepstakes, prosper and sing. And you, faithful reader, have a ball.

August Kleinzahler

Now winter nights enlarge
The number of their hours,
And clouds their storms discharge
Upon the airy towers

Let now the chimneys blaze
And cups o'erflow with wine;
Let well-tuned words amaze
With harmony divine

Thomas Campion,
Third Booke of Ayres

ROBERT BRINGHURST

Death By Water

It was not his face nor any
other face Narcissus saw
in the water. It was the absence there
of faces. It was the deep clear
of the blue pool he kept on
coming back to and that kept on coming
back to him as he went to it, shipping
out over it October after October
and every afternoon,
walking out of the land-locked summer,
out of the arms of his voice,
walking out of his words.

It was his eye, you may say,
that he saw there, or
the resonance of its colour.
Better to say it was what he listened for—
the light along the water, not
the racket along the stones.

Li Po too. As we do. And for the love of hearing
our voices and for the fear of hearing
our voices and those of the others come back
from the earth, we refuse to listen but look
down the long blue pools of air that come toward us and say
they make no sound, they
have no faces, see they have each other's eyes.

Ararat

The deepening scour of the keel across this
granular water.   Nothing more.   The fissure
through the estuary five thousand feet over the headwater.
These
         are the real mouths of rivers. The teeth,
not the slough and the rattles.

                              We have been here
before, eating raw air, but have always
forgotten,

all day eating the air the light
impales,
         stalking the singular animal.

    I no longer remember whether a fish
or a bird.   Nor whether its song or its silence
is what we were listening for.
                              I remember
a bow in a black tree, and a snowbound
ploughshare.
              Here is no spoor and no flotsam
timber.   Simply the blue sliding into
the furrow on the tilting light, and the violet
sky always casting the same white shadow.

Song Of The Summit

The difference is nothing you can see—only
the dressed edge of the air
over those stones, and the air goes

deeper into the lung, like a long fang,
clean as magnesium. Breathing
always hollows out a basin,

leaving nothing in the blood
except an empty
cup, usable for drinking

anything the mind finds—bitter
light or bright darkness or the cold
corner of immeasurable distance.

This is what remains: the pitted blood
out looking for the vein,
tasting of the tempered tooth and the vanished flame.

Jacob Singing

for Roo Borson and Joseph Keller

What I am I have stolen.
I have climbed the mountain with nothing in my hand
except the mountain. I have spoken to the god
with nothing in my hand except my other hand.
One against the other, the smith against the wizard,
I have watched them. I have watched them
wrestle one another to the ground.
I have watched my body carry my head around
like a lamp, looking for light among the broken stones.

What I am I have stolen.
Even the ingrained web
in the outstretched palm of this body,
limping on oracle finger and thumb,
dragging a great weight, an arm or a tail
like the wake of a boat drug over the ground.
What I am I have stolen. Even my name.

My brother, I would touch you but these
are your hands. Yours, yours though I call them
my own. My brother, I would hold your shoulders
but only the voice is mine. My brother,
the head is a hand that does not open
and the face is full of claws.

What I am I have stolen.
These mountains which were never mine
year after year have remade me.
I have seen the sky coloured with laughter.
I have seen the rocks between the withered water
and the quaking light. I have climbed the mountain
with nothing in my hand except the handholds
as I came upon them, leaving my hands behind.

I have eaten the sun, it is my muscle,
eaten the moon, it is my bone.
I have listened to the wind, whipped
in the heart's cup, slap and whistle in the vein.

My father said:
the wood will crawl into the apple,
the root will crawl into the petal,
the limb will crawl into the sepal
and hide.

But the fruit has eaten the tree, has eaten the flower.
The body which is flower and fruit together
has swallowed its mother, root and stem.
The lungs are leaves and mine are golden.

I have seen the crow carry the moon
against the mountain.
I have seen the sky crawl under a stone.

I have seen my daughter
carried on the land's shoulder.
I have seen the wind change
colour above her.
I have lain in silence, my mouth to the ground.

I have seen the light drop
like a wagon-sprag in the crisp stubble.
I have seen the moon's wheels
bounce through the frozen ruts
and chirp against the pebbles.
I have seen the metal angels
clatter up and down.

I have seen the flushed ewes
churn in the pen and the picked rams boil
against the hazel. I have seen them
strip the poplar, scrub the buckeye bare.
I have seen the mixed flocks
flow through the scented hills like braided oil.
I who never moved as they do.
I have climbed the mountain
one foot up and one hoof down.

The breath is a bone the flesh comes loose around.

Flower and fruit together.
But this other, this other
who is always in the body,
his lungs in my belly and
his head between my thighs.
O his arms go backward,
his legs go side to side.

My son, you have asked for a blessing. I give you
a blessing. I tell you,

The eye will flow out of the socket like water,
the ear will gore like a horn
and the tongue like another,
the sailor will stay in his house near the harbour,
the labourer, blinkered and fed will stay at his labour,
the soldier will soldier,
the lawyer will smile like milk and swill liquor,
the judge will glide like a snake keeping pace with the horses,
the man with gay eyes will like chocolate,
the roebuck will wrestle the air and you will hear music,
the rancher will prosper,
the wolf will walk out of your hand and his teeth will be shining.

But this one, my grandson, the young one,
this one will steal the eye and the tooth
of the mountain, this one will ride with his dogs
through the galleries of vision, this one will move
among the rain-worn shapes of men
with faces in his hands and the fingers writhing.
This one will slide his spade through the sea
and come away carrying wheat and linen.
This one, the young one, will steal
the sun and the moon,
the eye and the tooth of the mountain.
This one, the young one, how tall,
shaking hands and trading armour
with his dark-eyed brother.

My son, you must do more
than listen to the angel; you must wrestle him.
And one thing further: he must be there.
The muscle in the air, the taut light
hinged in the milky gristle
and the swollen dark, the smell
like the smell of a cornered animal.

I have oiled these stones to sharpen the wind.
I have come or I have gone, I have forgotten.
I hold what I hold
in this chiasma of the hands.

I have set my ear against the stones
and heard them twirling.
I have set my teeth against the stones
and someone said he heard them singing.

Hiatus

The weedy light through the uncurtained glass
Finds foreign space where the piano was,
And mournful airs from the propped-open door
Follow forlorn shreds of excelsior.
Though the towel droops with a sad significance
All else is gone; one last reviewing glance,
One last misplacing, finding of the key,
And the last steps echo, and fade, and die.
    Then wanderer, with a hundred things to see to,
Scores of decisions waiting on your veto,
Or worse, being made at random till you come
So weeks will pass before you feel at home,
Mover unmoved, how can you choose this hour
To prowl at large around a hardware store?
When you have purchased the superfluous wrench
You wander still, and watch the late sun drench
The fruit-stalls, pavements, shoppers, cars, as though
All were invisible and safe but you.
    But in your mind's ear now resounds the din
Of friends who've come to help you settle in,
And your thoughts fumble, as you start the car,
On whether somebody marked the barrel where the
    glasses are.

All Fools' Eve

From rooming-house to rooming-house
The toasted evening spells
City to hayrick, warming and bewildering
A million motes. From gilded tiers,
Balconies, and sombre rows,
Women see gopher-hawks, and rolling flaxen hills;
Smell a lost childhood's homely supper.
Men lean with folded newspapers,
Touched by a mushroom and root-cellar
Coolness. The wind flows,
Ruffles, unquickens. Crumbling ash
Leaves the west chill. The Sticks-&-Stones, this City,
Lies funeral bare.
Over its gaping arches stares
That haunt, the mirror mineral.
In cribs, or propped at plastic tablecloths,
Children are roundeyed, caught by a cold magic,
Fading of glory. In their dim
Cement-floored garden the zoo monkeys shiver.
Doors slam. Lights snap, restore
The night's right prose.
Gradually
All but the lovers' ghostly windows close.

The World Still Needs

Frivolity is out of season.
Yet, in this poetry, let it be admitted
The world still needs piano-tuners
And has fewer, and more of these
Gray fellows prone to liquor
On an unlikely Tuesday, gritty with wind,
When somewhere, behind windows,
A housewife stays for him until the
      Hour of the uneasy bridge-club cocktails
      And the office rush at the groceteria
      And the vesper-bell and lit-up buses passing
      And the supper trays along the hospital corridor,
Suffering from
Sore throat and dusty curtains.

Not all alone on the deserted boathouse
Or even on the prairie freight
(The engineer leaned out, watchful and blank
And had no Christmas worries
Mainly because it was the eve of April),
Is like the moment
When the piano in the concert-hall
Finds texture absolute, a single solitude
For those hundreds in rows, half out of overcoats,
Their eyes swimming with sleep.

From this communal cramp of understanding
Springs up suburbia, where every man would build
A clapboard in a well of Russian forest
With yard enough for a high clothesline strung
To a small balcony . . .

A woman whose eyes shine like evening's star
Takes in the freshblown linen
While sky a lonely wash of pink is still
reflected in brown mud
Where lettuces will grow, another spring.

Two Mayday Selves

The grackle shining in long grass
this first day of green casts
an orchid-mile of shadow
into the sun-meld, that marvel, those
meadows of peace (between the bird
and the curved curb
of the city-center clover-leaf).

The aloof
tiers of offices, apartments, hotels,
schools, park branches, opal
heaven-hidden stars, the other
beholder—out there, here,
insect-sing, a cappella,
the sticky welter—
brilliance, buds,

June bugs—
steam into globules
on the hill domed over the moles'
palaces. Knuckled winter
and its grease-stiff hood: where
is it still? is it past
any convulsive gulp, any least
whistling whisker-work
on the lush park
green, on the princely
bird and his glossiness
(reminiscent of flies) and the rice-
perfuming light sifting
between that pointing distance
and this?

"Old ghoul, leather-tough diaphragm,
listen!—I am
holding *my* breath.
The power of the blue and gold breadth
of day is poured out, flooding, all
over all.
Come out. Crawl out of it. Feel
it. You,
too."

Transit

Blowing hard at the bus stop:
south-bound, N.-W. corner.
Barometer falling.
Stars falling, but in that
blue sky who marks it, they fall all over out there.

Wind's off the Barren Straits.
But the sun is blowing too.
Reared high out of the nest
snakeheads flap in it till the
tear ducts crackle.

The whole geste unrolls; black cars,
poles, black-&-white headlines,
dentist's floss, wire-mesh,
heads spinning, and
a thorn needle for every solitary tune even though there's no
automatic arm. And it's
all plugged in
and everything's coming
But the bus isn't coming.

Noon keeps swallowing.

In Time

Stumps in the skull
feel smooth.
No juice. No punkwood.
Sheaves
of tall timber
sprout awkwardly—poplar clumps
        by the railway cut—
in a matter of years.

That's growth.

Smell the leaf-acid
in the new sky.

Natural/Unnatural

Evening tilt makes a
pencil-box of our
street.
The lake, in largeness, grapey blueness
casts back the biscuit-coloured pencil-box, boxes, toys, the
steeple-people, all of it, in one of those
little mirrory shrugs.

The north-east sky too
grows fuselage cool.

On the horizon
ghosts of peeled parsnips point their
noseless faces up,
out; ghost-bodies pile up on each other, all prone, all
pointless, blanking, refusing.

Even the west, beyond the tinged rooftops
smells of cobalt;

      "no—the
      charring of a peeled stick in a bonfire
      is the smell: newness,
      October crackling…"
large pink children have, all the same, sniffed
the ice in
that quirk of sunset
but refuse
fear.

There is still a lingering
sand-edge of sound
darkness explores.

In hope I say: it is a
listening into a
voice-sound, a voice making with silence.

"Hope is a dark place
that does not refuse
fear?"

> True, the natural night is pressure on my ribs:
> despair—to draw that in, to
> deflate the skin-pouch, crunch out the
> structure in one
> luxuriant deep-breathed zero—
> dreamed already, this is
> corruption.

I fear *that*.

I refuse, fearing; in hope.

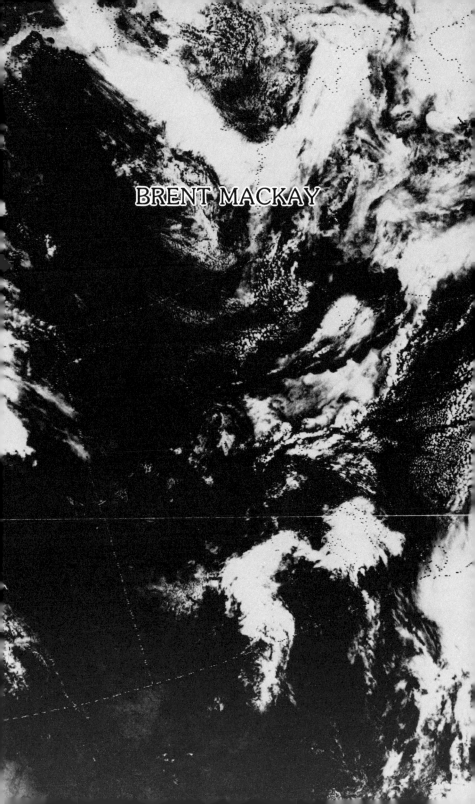

An Idle's Notes

Tokyo 1923

I

Dismal pillow.

Too much tea makes me sleepless.

As if living isn't stupid enough:
the wind in a catfight
like rush hour traffic.

At 3   small rivers in the gutters
        water under the walls.

The roof leaked.

II

Up late mad.

Down Silk Lane into Ginza

temple numb
                plumpit
throat
        my feet tingled

every eyeball
on a single thread
stitched to a swollen hump
a ribbon road

Cakes cracked, bricks swayed.
Plaster filled the air.

In a few seconds.
A rubbish heap in a few seconds.

III

When the first murmur comes
run quick midst bamboo
root that knits earth
or run to open ground
or hug the trunk of a hardwood tree

Streets heaps of rubble
People running higgledy piggledy like ants
I followed from jag to jag
I saw blue shirts
porpoises in rock
I stopped uselessly
someone yelled fire

Black smoke attacked sky

Dragons spat teeth

I weaved through into the park

Wind in the south
dirt my mouth.

IV

Years passed in hours,
faces feared nothing left but death.

Southwind veered stiff from West.

From Kudan Hill the whole city seemed hell.

I slept by the lake.

Gulls on rooftops
saki cups in moonlight
the monkey kettle puzzles kitchen steam
purple as dulce on a kitetail
fume and grain of skin

I moved near a group of men squatting round
a campfire picking pieces of meat. I sat.
I ate. I stuttered thanks and listened to
talk of assassinations. A great war. Of
mountains burning. How each would die.

V

Morning.

Northwind vapid with smell of ash
We stirred to hear an official report

Smoke curled in every corner

Half the city is gone
The princesses are both dead
The Emperor has ordered relief

Shootingstars on an empty slate

A girl in a torn dress
appeared like a goddess
through a sea mist

Who makes sense of it?

See the kiteflyers,

Letters birds write

Abortion

In an afternoon
of skillsaws and crowcaws
she sleeps chilled.

> 'She took my arm
> fragile pale
> wanting air'

Uncertain
birds watch cats
sun in sealaced air
puffing the curtain;
silent, distant
nausea aches
like cartires ache
pavement.

> 'Driving there
> something circled
> unseen above
> reluctant wavering'

Released
she wakes;
winter creeps
up the mountain.

Dining Out In Southern France

Two seats
(one each)
of two boards
one green
one grey
with a trace
of wine and green
on four stones
(two each)
where we eat
cucumber and munster
by scorched pine
sharp rock
above a traintrack
below an autoroute
a cafe of
two seats:
two boards
one sunbleached
mint green
one grey
with a trace
of rosé and
similar green
each on two stones:
host and hosted
lunar, alone.

Drayton Park

Not wept ripe
or rigid

a hand
resting
on a pelvis

without
thought
or control

like a bird
on a wall

melts
a pulse

of touch
weeping

sad moments
of flesh

fleeting
in a pigeon's
blink.

Not much more

this history
of skin
everlasting

spinning
in the smell

of a cigarette.

Uranos

Pubic clover private under olive
or fig growing yellow mid November
crushes like snow
under footsteps' tremor.

Trunks twist climate;
faces in the village
surrender years to all their tasks' temper;
season to season surpasses glamour
bent to wellrope
and unlevel tillage.

Sky grey as a knifeblade to lark's warble
divides life into whatever man knows
watching his winter wood kindle.

Oranges overhang mournful candles
lit in memory of faded photos
on important graves,
gravel or marble.

After Guido Cavalcanti

Fresca rosa novella,
pious primavera,
by park, river
your red soprano
I declare rarest
among la verdura.

Your finesse finishes
heartless or beardless men
in celebration;
birds are agog
evening and morning
for such latin:
arbutus words.
(Caledonia! Cincinnati!
Incant Cavalcanti!
Angel-creator).

Angel semblance
reposes in you;
(God what adventure
fuels my destiny)!
Your clear gaze
a passing advance
on nature's costume,
a miracle's cause.
Indeed fra-lore
calls you goddess:
nothing contrary
adorns your presence;
you alone describe natura.

Human nature's altar
you face the face of God
Flora Regina,
Wildrose Alberta,
Sweetwine Granada;
(don't be rude
to a villain of providence).
And if I'm a herring,
an outrageous datepit,
don't blast me:
love alone forces it
without manners
or doubt.

Ariadne

The season grasps
a handful
of ash
and grieves
the insubstantial seed
harassed to life
around a grave.

Breath invades
the weary,
the empty,
the stunned and distressed
besieged
by a heart's treason.

Fickle chimes
cross the mountain:
goatbells
in leeside thicket
or carobtree
fidget
reaching bud
and blossom.

I sat
in an olivegrove
without stratagem
or hope
when she came
on the same wind
fluttering
the butterfly
I watched
uncertain.

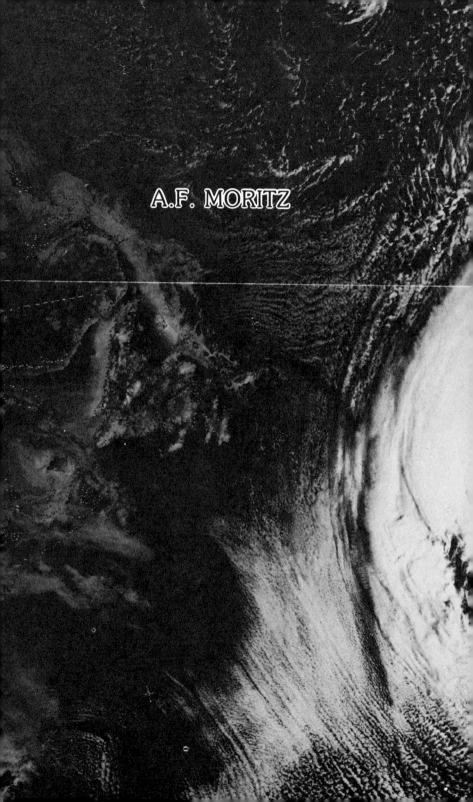

Permanence Of Evening

As I walked down the Rue Placide, Maria,
your half-made bed flew beside me
at the level of the third floor windows,
the milky inside of your left arm like the story
of a stupid romance and a botched suicide.

Until at the corner of the Piltdown Road
it collided with Luce-Elaine, that pillar
of smoky gardens; she always comes
to that corner to meet and guide me.

And the two of you fell together with the sound
of piles driven at another building start.
There is so much construction going on, the city
changes from one week to the next:
if I were blind I don't know how I would live here.

Thus all my former wives combine themselves
into daughters to be my brides, my brides
stand around like towers tacked through the joints
of a giant butterfly spread out on the ground.

The result of my laudable attempts
to 'deal boldly with substantial things':
the river is never the same, but then
it is never any different, and all I want
is to be awakened every moment by dawn
in a place no one's ever seen.

Second Person

To think of you is to dream.
You stand in the arch free of any wall
at the top of the crumbling stair
cut in the cliff side. Beyond you
the field returns heat to the sky
transformed with musk, men of foam
leaning on their elbows float
in the perfumed water, a go-between
light continually promotes desire,
and none of them are as naked as you are.

To look closely at you reveals
nothing but blood floating in milk,
the reminiscence of repeated disaster
delicately nursed. But this
is hard to remember, for your essential colour
is the pale gold fountain
that leaps between your fingers and your look.

'In the morning', you seem to say,
'you will find me in the woods,
asleep at the base of an oak tree.
At first you will catch a single gleam
and think it's a fallen sapling stripped of bark'.
But when we reach you, there's only a door
open at the verge of empty air.

These Dwarves

In the mornings I like things very clear
and these dwarves oblige me
like a firm stone island in a mudslide.
Among the paratroopers dropped by science
from above the clouds,
they are happy exhibiting their smoky stammers
that fog the edges of the well-honed leaves.
They are slower than a track
abandoned by all trains,
so slow that by merely being the whole world
blurs and burns itself in the friction of rushing past them.
For the traveller who catches sight of them,
they assume the expression of crows who have swallowed diamonds.
And from their bowels, the diamonds pronounce
the moves of a chess game,
and in the diamond language moan popular songs
which emerge in the crow language
as directions to a lost mine.
At dawn, however, these dwarves reveal themselves
as signposts the wind and rain have erased.
On their hunched backs they bear a spectrum
from coagulated purple to the sparsest orange,
and though sometimes they appear to move,
if anyone grasps their shoulders he touches wood.

Black Orchid

A black orchid convokes bees
at your body's centre,
a stem of urine
connects it to the ground.
Beside where you stand, the fishes
leap up an arc of light
and hang in a rainbow
over the disgorging cleft.

We are sad while we live here.
We hate this summer for the fleshy children
who force themselves as food into our eyes
closed toward the future.
Then the summer swells,
it will not last forever.
How we long for deliverance
as the lizards show and disappear
between the white rock
and the leaves: blue and green
little replicas of how the sky
like acid meets and etches
the temple of the palm forest.

And looking into the region
of that burning, with what desire
earth is moved
continually to pour itself.
The fountain raises its head
and with water's passionate vengeance
loses all
to colour the dry rock with these flowers.

The Air-Hammer

Stained with red, the leaves were blown down
on the compressor that forged the air into blows
for the hammer breaking up the road. The pieces
were heaped into trucks and sometimes still a stretched
artery of tar linked one to another.

Children here, we slept in one room
where now the submachine gun rattle
attacks concrete. The nearness then
of your mystery, one day to be mine,
displayed but never divulged:
its skeletal image remains in me
of a soft human cleft in granite.

Will we at least be blown
against each other once again,
clenched in the same sweep
of a grey sky's trailing net?

In the vicinity of our childhood
houses diminish, vacant lots expand
and the days do nothing,
only hands work, conveying through idle time
bricks of the stairways, bridges, walls.

They are poured into hopper cars
and taken to the designated place
and there poured into pits.
Where water attacks the firmness of the land,
they support foundations
and good offices stand on the swamp.

The people who clean those buildings by night
swarm now from the district of our birth.
And here when they return
at dawn, the air-hammer
crumbles and quarries their sleep.

Signs And Certainties

Look for the time when in the woods
the walnut tree will dress herself
in the fashion of flowers
and perfume her head and neck;
if her fruit overwhelms you
with the sight and the thought of it,
later in the year the grain too
will be overwhelming
and the overburdened threshing
come in an abundant heat.
But if poor in fruit
she spreads herself into leaves
and covers the ground with shadows deeper
than black water, then the straw—
nothing but chaff—will be pounded
on the floor with no result.
And I have seen the farmer's pods,
though bred long and with great care,
still fall and rot on the ground
unless year after year the man
picks off the largest. So everything
falls backward, runs from much to less,
as a rower in a strong river,
if he relaxes for a moment,
is swept down toward the sea.

Stage Magician

Squads of eyes blunt helpless
.Against a cabinet swords enter
And withdraw: control rods to fulminate applause.
Familiar wine pours
From empty cups. And always
The random assistant
Boxed, sliced, scattered, rejoined.
But, should hand stutter in its saltarello,
Cuff lay one egg—all is lost.

All depends on crisp lapel
And luminous glove, licensed livery
Of the immaculate deceit
Whose audience, unspotted by blush or conspirator's grin,
Close round to urge
His draped unconscious woman
Lift like a window blind
On our packed horizon: mouths monocled in gape
Where blear stars of souls dawn.

Astrologia

The stars: a compass natant
in cold alcohol sky.
This to preserve their definition, crisp.
Yet, how shifted, imperceptibly,
the whole vast demijohn of night,
borne elliptically to a Smithsonian back shelf.

Maintenance is maintained,
dust is feathered from the glass shoulders.
An attendant pressed frequently to change
the clouding fluid
finds the spirits penetrate
these orbs, even as eggs are pickled.
Together they gray.

Nightly his stations multiply,
fixtures, artifacts and signs agitate
for lives of their own, demand
waxed observance. Rare it is
from the great jar he washes free
a calendar of oily skin,
and slow admires, with trouble turning,
the container on his lap
till day releases him.

Artifacts

Content among kitchen wares at last
to scour my traces with hard blue dust
till your reflection indifferent sings —stainless.
Yet as these tailings wash to me,
I sift, groom and care for
rude implements and sainted bone,
trinkets of antiquity.

Alone, one reliquary holding I repent:
this Janus-mask, however worn,
slack-jawed, blank as stone,
is shaped on the child's astonishment.

Blackberry Chronicle

Spring
      summer
            after love's passing
after undulate acres of leaf
demulcent as cricket wings
scuffing green on green
give way; the slow acid rain
of blackberries unpicked

spreads an earth-poultice,
scours the nostril's sanctuary.

If clouds were Zeppelins,
then these, their flamed-out skeletons.
Through gray bone-loops, weaponed, guarding
clear spaces
the wind moves:
through love-distorted sheets
torn and singing.

Giuoco Piano

I didn't expect when first we played
this fuss, this grandmaster's seriousness,
too much friends for a friendly game.
I didn't see a tournament
with rules: touch, and you must move,
while in alternate gulps
a timer drains us.

Negligent with handling
the pieces red, white,
smudge one uniform
sweat and pigment.
Now, my worthy, the test of skill,
resist early stalemate, random carnage.
How dedicated with only the reticle
to suggest: This can be playable?

Restraint, decorum,
observance of form if not direction.
A striking move is made —against whom?
The judges fight and memory
quick with first colours
(Apple Red, Eve White)
is humoured then ignored
while armies press and yield
exotic symmetries across the board.

Be it known, as pieces pair then fall,
survivors gain a virtue from the dead
no agreement for a draw should mollify.
Pink must win, not you, not I.

Solar Probe II

Over the shrunk labyrinth, Icarus gloating
missed the beeswax trickle of his wing
and moulted in the summer sun.
But we respect the micro-maze, circuits
finer, we trust, than spider's lace.
A naked bird's an ugly thing.

A sidereal dial face, this window
is no crystal sphere;
luminous conventions of awe remain
like up and down
in phase with our needs.

And when we pierce the plasma of this star
where conga lines of protons
marathon the circuit's load,
our breakers burp the quanta of survival
to fling us intact to an anxious town.

Transmigration

Kafka, reluctant to drink Lethe
without his notebooks sent along
sips Vichy for his phantom limbs,
complains his lot was drawn in haste:
      Offspring of a phoenix and ptarmigan?
      Parents, what business with each other,
      how was this marriage chaste?

On a nest of ash
persistent as a defunct crater
rain steams an answer:
      Our bodies we led to each other, absently
      let them play, two witless children
      and back to the heady feast had barely turned...

Nest of ash. Cinnebar egg
perspiring incubation's silver oil; hatched
neither here nor there. Hybrid,
plagued with chronic fever
feathers fuse crustaceous,
wings cup to body, lift
and close.
Mollusc-wings
pump the viscin dreams
thin oxygen, as if, in kiting north
he seeks the temperate
in gelid squalor,
an Arctic branch of The Worker's Accident Insurance
where pipelines shunt inter-office memos
and refineries bloom like grain-fed
interiors of dictaphones.
Here he remains, to quern policy, query indemnity
from all the frost-brittle machines
where flesh, moist, not invigilant,
sticks like meringue.

Night Snack

A slow pull on the door, a wedge jumps free,
an expanded ghost of lemon pie
drags my kitchen into yellow particulars.
But I am hungry —stray light pales
before the refulgence of operating theatres.

A scalpel flashes:
before me on a rack, lit from underneath and above:
the surviving fragments of our conjunction.
A planetarium. They revolve,
offer themselves for swallowing and digestion.
They shudder; a compressor somewhere begins.
Absently, tubes varicose direct intrusive heat
to where pipes struggle lost
in their jacket of glass hair.

Is this real hunger? The grapes are sour,
bisquits have sucked up all precursing savours,
the brie weeps uncontrollably, like time itself
the wedge of lemon
shrinks to a suture.

Shownman

To me the rifle has ever been mightier than the pen.

I

Archie Belaney Grey
Owl

not Mohawk Oneida
Onondaga
Cayuga Seneca or Tus-
carora not Iroquois

neither Five nor Six
Nations
            never no Huron

Jicarilla Apache

Montagnais nope
Napaki
Cree
Têtes de Boule nor
Penobscot Mic-
mac nor Wabanaki

by adoption Ojib-
way and truly
Wa-Sha-Quon-Asin
Algonkian Lon-
duck or Chippeway

the chrysalis moot
British Tex-
Mex Scot or
Canuck

the son of Katherine
Cochise or Cox and Mac-
Neil a rake or hero
friend of Buffalo
Bill's or fan

born at Hastings or Hermo-
sillo   Bear
Island   Lake
Ajawaan

It's never late
til morning

and then it's
early.

II

Archibald Stansfeld Belaney changed
his name, race and serial
number

            faded into dense bush

            emerged river-born
guiding a divinity
student in the bow of his canoe

            no clashing of cymbals
            but the roaring dictate
            of the rapids taught this
            seminarian
his first lesson in fear-of-the-lord

            so throwing down
                        the paddle
he clasped hands in
                        supplication

              shite and
              white water

Grey Owl, "Quit your fool
              babbling and get that paddle, man,
          when you're in my
                  canoe I
am your Lord".

III

Bad Hat

the young hellion balanced
hatchet prowess with Shake-
speare and Browning the accent on
throwing-knives and like stunts

the girls must go home
giddy from dancing to Archie's
piano and drum fandangoes his
fingers' touch still tight on their
ribs their perfume and whiskey blanc
still high in his nose

the station agent and The Bay
factor pasted and frightened
the Law down from Chapleau
the strangers who laughed out of line
the old citizens who required
their peace

made him brood

he was never penitent
always the bloody knives or the Browning
got him in trouble in town
when he left there he shot at both churches
two bells in their steeples rang from his bullets

IV

Too-True-Tall-Tales

I'll walk across Algonquin Park in the dark
and I'll carry my gun all the way
I'll do it in the freezing
night if I can't get across in a day
and I'll do it cold
          light no blessed fire
drawing rangers to catch me when I tire

you bet — I'll dare and
              I'll collect

              But the goddam ice was thin
and like the greenhorn I haven't been
since 17 I stepped in it past my boot
alright   past my bloody knee.

Then I went fast though the leggings
freezing chafed the skin of my groin
and my toes went numb   too right
       my feet   I couldn't feel
I was falling off my very snowshoes

but I kept my gun

and I kept travelling
and never lit no fire
though I could've and might as well've
because yes he picked up my trail

'twas a rumour
              he caught, mind,
                        never a scent

he found me too and I thank him and Him twice
I'd drifted asleep with that peculiar
sleep you may fall into only once a life.

Ho, part cat I am, with eight lives I left
his ranger's roost after a fortnight
and not a toe did I lose

til I left my traps and went to trenches
and Jerry shot 'em off in the Great War.

Hell, them bastards
only ever got me by accident.

V

The Trigger in the Trees

        cuss softly
only at trivia that breath
be saved

        squeeze
the trigger in the trees

        burn the beaver's
knees to make amends
        put tobacco in the bear
skull's brain-pan
        hang him on a limb to witness
man's poor awe

hard years to learn
seasons' easy lessons

the best thing you can do in summer
is marry
fight fire or show Americans where
pike bask

pray for bitter winters: cold
best conditions ice and
snow for shoe and toboggan

ignore the dying black and yellow
            eyes the bloody forearms
admire the flayed sable fur

                            then
where the disappearing creatures could be
found to kill my wife refused to follow

A wed woman and a caught
lynx conspired.
The Beaver People wanted
much. They made live
music.

The cudgel started turning in my hands.

Bewildered, our eyes
began to meet in Silent Places

saints and man conversed at mid-
night and noon of earthly
ways and profanity

                traps'
weight drowns
                creation

        he hefts a pencil
to trace the Past for vice and assent

                    *   *   *

    ... these writings that were no longer mine,
but which I now saw only as recorded echoes
and not creations of my own, had captured ...
the essentials of what had eluded me so long.
    And I felt at last that I had been made to
understand.

VI

Alba: England

All night I'll stand til day
breaks and from dawn
I'll stand til the day begins.

I'll prove all the patience of a life-
time in the pitch dark hours
men dream through.

Snowblind, I could find
the cover of the pines
by ear and stand the storm
til Neganikabo came before
and struck that fire.

I can with foreboding
behold my fame
unproclaimed. Perhaps come morning
that publisher entrusts
me with the lore a writer
needs to live in London?

VII

People like a Forest
                    listening   .

lecterns fit the hand as thwart
                    and haft

applause like relief at the end of a carry
heavy in increments of disillusion

backstage they beg,
                    Please be
"Saint-Francis-of-the-Beavers"
and the appeal of a woman with a knowing
eye is great. A fool's fists are flies.
A water-glass full of whiskey, if you
please

The obscure woods are better.
Oathes keep better.
That pilgrimage would be good to make
again

but oh God

the forest back down
the way none may go

there the only
nourishment and service

now

        the land and family
        finally estranged

VIII

At A Command Performance
                              the performer
readies himself on stage at the pleasure
                              of the royal
entourage
                    when he has waited
Their Majesties enter.

He may never relax.

Noblesse Sauvage n'oblige personne.

                    You, Your
                    Majesties,
                    be seated
                    first

                    then command
                    my entrance.

                    I will not keep you waiting.

                    I will be there
                    instanter.

                    *   *   *

As the princesses bid me
I will linger: the children hear
my tales of the Height of Land in
storied Far Away where the water
falls white as age from eminence
to eminence...

we will take tea in frocks and buckskins
then say farewell
and I will clap their father on the shoulder
and call him brother.

IX

"I can be good company", Grey Owl
sighed
        where he had no company.

Anahareo's tenderness saves us
when we might fight; saves us
like the Bedouins, the Arab Lawrence led.

A woman on the CP line through Biscotasing
showed my brother old scars Archie gave her
with the point of his knife. She remembers him
taking to the wild.
He was not apostate;
he never was converted. Her eyes twinkle;
invite memory.

how to survive midwinter nights
with a single blanket, a lean-to
of boughs and a small fire? how to
stay alive all those hours?:

still my questions:
how to travel the rapids / by night
how to trap at all?

"I live for the small, 'live things.
They are my living, to whom
I credit my life. Their pelts
are worth more than yours and mine.
Still, Sir, I bow to you and, Madame,
I am charmed".

ALEXANDER HUTCHISON

Flyting

'for all this
and all that

and nature
        sparking
at my elbow'

This is for emptiness
this is for gluttony

this is for mawkishness
thrashed to a foam

this is for blisters
on sisters in whirlwinds

for all those who need
to slide closer to home

This is slash-burning
to upstart opinion

each vice vouchsafed
each virtue sublime

invention exhausted
though scarcely invented

'the work of the self
in sufficiency of time'

This is for thin change
and careful advances

this is for fuckit
and do as you please

this is for fine words
that butter no parsnips

creeping to heaven
on well-padded knees

This is a labyrinth
hedged in with simony

nosing in circles
to subtle intent

this is for chalky thighs
speckled like sausages

grinding the teeth
of an old discontent

This is for namelessness
this is for avarice

this is for lunging
to deathless renown

this for necessity
razoring chances

howling and hounded
like bears around town

This gives the gist of it
this takes the sting from it

'one thing goes pulsing
then everything does'

this is specific
for whatever ails thee:

Go take up serpents
use beeswax and buzz.

This is for *mousikè*
this is for *technè*

in fire-hail
and fire-flaught

the word has come down

namelessness brainlessness
boasting an accolade

this is for trumpery
sparking a crown

This one will harrow them
garlic and bryony

Blocking and Grudging
and Pecking Apart

this is new testament
flinty then fluvial

saltires and salvoes
to uncluttered art.

In Brass And In Brimstone I Burn Like A Bell

Nearing the beast that baits:
Things close to the heart.
                    ('First
You remember the fox scattered russet
Before me, pelting down the Old Woman
So fast I had to keep running or else
Hit and stay put')

    Clammer of stones loud as blood;
    A moon more skin than shell
    To full eclipse.

Coming one with a shears and one with a bill-hook;
A boy with a glass of golden oil; chandler of hooks,
His nets hung like curtains; some wild and bewildered;
Some hawless, rank as a rake—

    'My hounds tore out my lady's life,
    But she stood bright upstanding'

—Phebus (for his brilliant hair) scorns
Those without malice on an easy *slauwe,*
Those drawing forfeit,

Backing off from real work like a horse
Backing off from a fire.

And the ringing of the game
As that which comes softly,
                    past hindrance,
By silent questing—

    Swallows in a knot of air
    Herring in a knot of water:
    A great unravelling of silver fish
    And silver birds

They would have love something other
That would have love whole.

A Slate Rubbed Smooth

Chronicle of the hunter of forms:
Of the white stag killed in the off-eye; grain struck
   dropped from the husk.
Given the distinction between what one does and what one is.
Between the world ignored and reckoned new;
Between perfect technique and perfect attunement;
Between this here now and everything else.

Willow and river-sand, rain-bangled water.
By Grantown fleet and Rothes to Fochabers' iron bridge
And bothies tar-streaked by Tugnet at the mouth
Sheer the Spey shifts.
Wind flattens grey-headed grasses,
Gulls lag or lapse to a sable sea.

Looking back to real beginnings, felicitous,
When the mind goes like a skipping stone across the water,
Planets at each dip, sun and simple air at every rise—
That man the master of hawks enjoyed his land free,
Had a hand-breadth of wax-candle to feed his birds
And light him to bed.

When he hunted, hawk and hunter shared the prey.

Climacteric

This time something threatens to give way entirely:
Ridgepole, roofbeam, whatever you imagine as lasting
This time will fail to remember words that fell so bright
And fast about we found no shelter but the storm itself.

Burning branches in stoves and stalls, juniper burning
And the place thick with the smell of it. Star-bane;
Lesion in the thew of space.

Even the confidence of God at knell of the hardest season
Withers and rots away.

These purposes splinter in a rented room:
Intention, surface, prospect before, behind
Is all some thriftless illusion
Drawn down in a trough of queer air.

I can guess at it—tailing, diminished,·
Acknowledge a thread of worn profit,
Even an infection slowly taken—

Nature scourged by sequent effects:
No lamp of bronze, no drum
At the cross-tree—
                    Appetite
And intelligence and little else;
Blood loop on a dry beaten run.

Traces

To see the first signs of the time: the seed-chap;
The way water travels beyond the reach of rivers and man.
Beginning with a thing converted; an equal mind in the face
    of blind contingency.
Beginning with the recognition of fact as a start for music.
Beginning with the eye and a sea-space.

Silver cars and copper—prows of silver and steel
Clap foam-flecks, heave bramble by stump.

Currents of scrub, great furrows of ebbing tide
Swivel to east, to pillars of woodland,

Jut of the pier-spiling rutted by spindrifts of light.

Nothing is inveterate: the direst habit of wind or
    circumstance wears new.
Even mockery or violent revenge—'That Roman in the Wall—
The stink of him—stewing from bracken, pile after pile.'
Beginning with bigotry and a degraded church;
A bone injured and decaying in the arm.
Beginning with gas, primordial, incandescent.
With a haggard hawk loosed from its traces.

It was to end with sea: a dark green swell,
Morning wind blowing gorse-smell and camomile
    to the ships brought round
To the anchorage of summer we had found—

Sloughed like a napkin one bird posts past reach
Coasts listlessly down by wave as you wade there
Something like sunlight, something like skin.

The Shrug, The Hum, Or Ha

Anoint the slug with salt or lye:
His appetite's a spattle trail
Before the slicks of mind and eye.

Tie fat on a limb for the sky:
So let it hang for jigget birds
Beyond the jinks of mind and eye.

Sparking spittle, fat and lye,
Slicks and jinks of mind and eye,
Spur, branch, and scauper's cry,
I light a start of calumny.

ACKNOWLEDGEMENTS

The following poems have appeared previously:

Robert Bringhurst: "Ararat" and "Song Of The Summit" in *Bergschrund* (Sono Nis); "Song Of The Summit" in *Cadastre* (Kanchenjunga); "Jacob Singing" in *Queen's Quarterly*, and as a Kanchenjunga Chapbook; "Death By Water" in *Malahat Review*, and as a Broadside from the U.B.C. Library.

Margaret Avison: "All Fools' Eve", "Hiatus", "The World Still Needs", in *Winter Sun* (U. of T. Press); "Two Mayday Selves", "Transit", "In Time", "Natural/Unnatural" in *The Dumbfounding* (Norton).

Brent MacKay: "Dining Out In Southern France" in *Montemora*.

A.F. Moritz: "Black Orchid", "These Dwarves", "Second Person" in *Black Orchid* (Dreadnaught); "These Dwarves" in *Bartleby's Review:* "Second Person" in *Dalhousie Review:* "Permanence Of Evening" in *New Poems* (Swan Books) and *Poetry Toronto.*

Guy Birchard: section IX of "Shownman" in *Brick.*

Alexander Hutchison: "Flyting" as a broadsheet from Barbarian Press: "Climacteric" in *Stand,* Vol. 16, no. 1, reprinted by permission of its editors; all the poems except "Flyting" are reprinted by permission of the publisher from DEEP-TAP TREE by Alexander Hutchison (University of Massachusetts Press, 1978), copyright © by Alexander Hutchison.

Thanks to Mr. S.A. Sauer, Curator of the Map Library at the University of Western Ontario, for permission to print the satellite photographs.